OXFORD POETS 2001

The editors of this anthology are members of the Oxford*Poets* Board.

David Constantine is an authority on Hölderlin, as well as a poet and translator. His most recent collection is *The Pelt of Wasps* (Bloodaxe, 2000).

Hermione Lee, Goldsmiths' Professor of English Literature at Oxford and Fellow of New College, is author of *Virginia Woolf* (1996) and other biographical and critical works.

Bernard O'Donoghue was born in Co. Cork in 1945. He teaches Medieval English at Wadham College, Oxford and has published four books of poems of which the most recent is *Here Nor There* (Chatto, 1999).

Oxford*Poets* 2001

an anthology edited by
David Constantine, Hermione Lee
and Bernard O'Donoghue

Oxford*Poets*
CARCANET

First published in Great Britain
in 2001 by
Carcanet Press Limited
4th Floor, Conavon Court
12-16 Blackfriars Street
Manchester M3 5BQ

A CIP catalogue record for this book
is available from the British Library

ISBN 1 903039 52 5

The publisher acknowledges financial
assistance from the Arts Council of England

Set in 10pt Palatino by Bryan Williamson, Frome
Printed and bound in England by SRP Ltd, Exeter

Contents

Introduction

Oxford Poets 2000 was a notable success. (It won a Poetry Book Society Recommendation, for example.) In this second anthology we continue in our original enterprise, which is to publish a good variety of interesting and lively new work.

This time we have nearly twice as many poets, and a greater mix of newcomers and others already well established either in the old Oxford list or elsewhere. The juxtapositions are striking. Altogether, the range of this anthology – in provenance, poetic dialect, subject and technique – is very wide.

The collection further demonstrates the qualities we admire. We want urgency; lively apprehension; and the patience, and the necessary craft, to convert merely personal insights and experiences into effective poems. We like poems that manifestly deal with things that matter. Such things are everywhere around us – in science, in politics, in private happiness and grief. The poems assembled here are proof of that.

Individually and as a group the Oxford Poets already make a distinctive contribution to modern verse. This anthology increases the contribution, and promises more.

JANE DRAYCOTT

Jane Draycott was born in London in 1954 and studied Medieval English Literature at Bristol University. She now lives and teaches in Oxfordshire. Her first two collections, *No Theatre* (Smith/ Doorstop) and *Prince Rupert's Drop* (Carcanet/Oxford), were both shortlisted for the Forward Prize in 1997 and 1999, and with poet Lesley Saunders and artist Peter Hay she is co-author of *Christina the Astonishing* (Two Rivers Press 1998).

Of the poems in this anthology, 'Because tonight the beach' first appeared in the *Times Literary Supplement*. 'Public Records Office' and 'No. 3 from Uses for the Thames' were both written as part of a Southern Arts residency at the River & Rowing Museum, Henley and first appeared in the *Bridport Prize Anthology 2000* and *Regatta Magazine*. 'Field Hospital' was first published in *Oxford Poetry*.

Because tonight the beach

Because tonight the beach will consider its life,
its lack of a future, tree hair thinning
and tree heart turning to stone or splinters of ice

they will arrive now, the snow girls, swimming in
from their islands, weightless detonations of paper or marble
or light, casting no shadows and wearing no shoes.

Not asking what country, whose footsteps or features or fable,
they'll travel together like raiders, sending the ghosts
of previous weather curling across the dunes,

feathering stonework and fences, their deepening presence
an absence, a plainness of speech laid on car parks and lawns,
a glimpse of a possible future, making a difference

to everything, this arrival of strangers, now –
familiar, unblemished, and just the right age for snow.

Public Records Office

*'If you would see something quite dreadful, go to the enormous palace
in the Strand, called Somerset House . . . What can men do in such a catacomb?'*
Taine – Notes sur l'Angleterre

Ink comes in on the tide and with the watermen
and moths cut up the stairs. Witnesses crowd
the courtyard in pairs, details are lost in the rain.

Behind the dead windows darkness is swallowing
the *Aula lucis*, the hall of light, like a sword:
year by year, marriage by marriage, a steady hand.

Last night, another murder in the watergardens.
Torches doused, the facts sit in pools on the flags
and that blind old allegory the Thames refuses to speak.

No mention here of those unaccountably let off
the hook, of the dates they were not with their friends
in the runaway hackneys, the train wrecks

or warships which broke like a biscuit, cordite
gangfiring back like a family tree through torpedo room,
ocean, the North Sea, past sandbanks and home.

In the river, the house and its offices hang like a ship
smeared with soot and the memory of flame underwater.

The Surgeon

He swims just before dawn, breasting the river
like a hill, parting it with his arms like a dancer
or priest. Ahead, a flat line of light divides the two
dark halves of the world from each other.

The air leans up close to his face and with
his ears only he senses the dark landscape
of the water, its prostrate fields and struggling hedges,
its low-lying ridges and flooded verges.

Below the surface, pearls of half-light, silver
with oxygen, cling like prayer beads to his fingers.
He is thinking about the anatomy of the heart,
the forks in the road, the red caves and narrow lanes

and on the horizon the possibility of a cathedral,
the sun rising like a corpuscle, winter wheat.

No. 3 from *Uses for the Thames*

'Feather!' cried the Sheep . . .
Lewis Carroll, *Through the Looking-Glass*

The test was to dip
the needles into the dark
of the swallowing mirror

and by pulling to row
the weight of your own small self
through the silvery jam of its surface

trailing behind in your passing
your very own tale, knitted
extempore from light

and then to lift them,
feathered, ready for flight.

Blue

Some thought they heard *flight*, others
that *fight* was the syllable uttered
on the floor of the forest, the young man
far from home, unable to tell us even his name.

All afternoon those among us convinced
they knew the root of a word when they saw it
argued the toss between *agony* and *ecstasy*

the green of his jacket the whole while dividing,
bursting towards the light, his mouthful of soot
spat upward in a fountain of feathers or leaves.

Night fell. We bent to the bones, hoping to hear
like the Bible translated against all laws
some sounds we might more easily swallow.
Kneeling, we listened.

Set like a net

Set like a net for the shadows of telegraph poles
falling over themselves to get home before dark,
this old system of fields receives its dead.

Raising themselves like light, the circus people
imagine themselves, sewing on stars, walking
the wires, crossing the high path to safety.

The news will barely have reached us before it's all over,
the juggling of children and plates, the throwing of torches,
the hanging of fathers and sons by their feet in the spotlight.

In the hedgerows the old men fine-tune their breath
to a filament, listening in to the silence of travellers
catching each other, putting a hand out tonight.

after a painting by Christopher Hedley-Dent

The Guava Path

Suppose you are contemplating an island.
It is not any island known to you . . .
Jill Paton-Walsh, *Knowledge of Angels*

Above him the blue, and the fist of the forest
pulling the darkness into itself like a handkerchief.
Weighed in the balance one foot is as good
as the other, but day is always better than night.

All this madness leaves the boy cold –
the reddening pathways, foreign and uncontrolled,
the morning's outright humidity, the village
free-falling behind him, forgotten already.

He is climbing the stairs to the rock which faced
with the sea is a child, has waited up for him all night.
He would like to lie down there, to sleep like a baby
right through the day, but knows that all he can do

is stare at the wall for sight of the girl
when she comes, of the ship which will move
like an institution, an impossible knot on a silken cord
bringing her to him, making them known to everyone.

Not the sky but the sea. Not the me but the you.
Not the I but the we. Not the blue but the blue.

Nobody saw them
for Sandra

Nobody saw them, or noticed the line they made
just by walking, their red shoes and things they had written
thrown down behind them like stones or pieces of bread.

Not the men they passed in the half-dark injecting the road,
not the bears, not even the wild woman, mother of seven,
not the huntsman on his road back to the palace alone.

No one recorded their trail through the long grass and quicksands,
the towpaths and stairwells, how some fell into the fens
or disappeared backwards through hedges without making a sound

how approaching a village or hilltop their little hearts rose
at the prospect ahead, unaware what had already happened –
the china already destroyed by the bull, the shop now closed.

So when the time came, it was only the birds in the trees
who saw their reflection: a window left open, a gap in the leaves.

Field Hospital

Each sheet has its own length.
A few are only a short afternoon,
others stretch for what seems like an eternity
all the way to the fence and the several
remaining fields just visible beyond.

Packets of trapped voices pass overhead
held in the shifting nets of the rain.
Lying in the cool straightforward grass
no one can see their toes, or needs to:
the horizontal wraps them up and delivers them

to the sky who will say *Yes, lie down, sleep
and I will observe you, for as long as it takes.*

Cockermouth Boy

In the museum's volcanic dark light dark
the stuttering boy raises the aerial of his arm
and offers to read: *And – in the – frosty – season,*
pushing the blades of the words out across
the surface of the morning, left right left,
each iron phrase a forward movement of himself.

Outside, the rain wheels and fills the conduits
and lakes, gathering like wax. *All – shod with – steel
we hissed – along the – polished – ice,* the schoolboy
pitching the whole body of his intonation into the skirts
of the wind, each sound caught, delayed, relayed.

Behind him, close to his ear, the poet's arcing skates
and sunlight, pooled in the mouth of the clouds.

ROBERT SAXTON

Robert Saxton was born in Nottingham in 1952, and read English at Magdalen College, Oxford. He currently lives in North London, and works as the editorial director of an illustrated book publishing company. He is a regular contributor to *Poetry Review*, and his poems have also appeared in *PN Review*, the *TLS*, the *Observer*, *Thumbscrew*, *Tabla*, the *London Magazine*, and elsewhere. His first collection, *The Promise Clinic*, was published by Enitharmon (1994). He has a new collection, *Bottomfishing*, ready for publication. In June 2001 he won the Keats-Shelley Prize (Poetry) for 'The Nightingale Broadcasts'.

Of the poems in this anthology, 'The Breakfast Cup' is based on five lines of a letter written by Elizabeth Bishop to Harold Leeds (15 August, 1979; published in *One Art*, her selected letters edited by Robert Giroux, Pimlico 1996).

The Six-Spot Burnet

Every flawless day has a present to offer,
Like the moth this afternoon in its kimono,
Fluttering green forewings, six red spots

On each shoulder, red hindwings, flambeau
Of soft fire over our field of knapweed.
The wings beat fast but the flight is slow.

Though lazy and easily taken, the six-spot
Burnet is fearless, because full of cyanide.
Every flawless day has a present to offer.

The Bittern

Shy, fat bird in a forest of brown stalks,
You stretch yourself to heaven tall and lean.
Even a giant so still could not be seen,

No more than could a falcon fast as light.
Safe as only the endangered are,
You intimate close secrets from afar,

Mile-off diversions at a fowler's feet.
To know if there's an iceberg in the room,
Stop talking. Listen for the foghorn's boom.

Life List
Red-throated diver

In the northernmost isles where Russians outdrink Norwegians
  and many a shore-bound wife has changed hands for a netful
                                        of cod,
  where oil people in donkey jackets caked with storm petrel shit
  play poker with cards so oil-stained,
  so abraded by salt-roughened hands, so vodka-fuddled,
  quarrels, often violent, sometimes to the death,
  arise over the suit, never mind the rank or number,
  so that some have simplified the pack to black and red,
  picture and plain,

divers breed on the lochans.

The Breakfast Cup
i.m. Elizabeth Bishop (1911–1979)

My 'student' had just left, I was searching irritably in the kitchen
  for his breakfast cup, when I heard through the part-open
  window the long groan of a tractor, maybe two tractors,

grazing the spruces like industrial deer, the annual mow,
  gear changes like the lurching of a plane, the heart
  or hearts in the cockpit free-falling in panic or bravado.

All the bees, hornets, wasps, and blueflies of North Haven
  were gathered up in that drone, though I could see a pair
  of broody iridescent blueflies bouncing above the sill,

where suddenly behind the drape I found the breakfast cup –
  why *put* it there? – then glimpsed a dirt-caked tractor
  cresting the ridge, familiar shock of dirty white hair,

whereupon this thought occurred to me: the old so-and-so,
  eighty a few weeks ago, would not remember what I'd said
  about the cranberry patch, or not till I strode up there,

wiping my hands on my apron. Nor would Dick Bloom,
   who'd brains enough but let his concentration roam
   like a bumblebee from one blowzy thing to another.

Later, they mowed around me as I picked – always keeping
   a neighborly distance, thumbs-up every now and then,
   and young Dick doffing his hat with a grand, sweeping

flourish, as if saluting me in the bank on Main Street –
   to win the admiration of some pretty girl, of course.
   Now I'm making quite a batch of lingonberry sauce.

North Haven, Maine – 15 August 1979

A Fox in the Cemetery

Beneath revetted tons of stone, a sleeping corm,
Layers uncrumpling in warm rain-fed little springs –
The European angel, northern race, the angel of the storm,
Who'll one day wrap these bones in full-grown wings.

A scientist lectured on the twenty types of pain
And won from Darwin and from Darwin's friends
A smattering of warm applause, a freshening rain,
Which fed a pamphlet's roots, and almost made amends.

Then mile by mile his map of pain turned red.
He became landscape, imagination flipped on its head,

Absorbed into other lives, petrified by local history,
Patience and pride, a stone replica angel on show,
Like a cormorant far out at sea lifting its wings to dry
In darkening storm-trapped light. The fox left hours ago.

MAUREEN DUFFY

Maureen Duffy was born in 1933 and educated at King's College, London. Her collections of poetry include *Evesong* (1975), *Memorials of the Quick and the Dead* (1979) and a *Collected Poems* (1985). She has published sixteen novels and plays for radio, TV and the stage, as well as several works of criticism and biography. Her most recent book, *England the Making of the Myths*, was published in March 2001.

Of the poems in this anthology, 'Eirlys' and 'Salvage' were first published in *Oxford Review*.

Revenant

A quarter century on your ghost comes haunting back
squats on the blacker strip of verge picked out
by the headlights and I scramble again
ungainly after as you scuttle away
just as you did before, only this time
I don't come back in the frosty dark
to find you dropped askew, eye dulled. The guns
have been out all day cracking the frozen
silence. As you run from me one wing
tries to lift the other warped close
to the curve of your back. Pest, vermin
crop stuffer, country cousin yet smart
suited in your rose waistcoat, black tie
morning coat, unlike that poor townee
a car once slammed into my path, only
the unmourning stars will see you go out
your plump puffball kicked aside by the shot
while I sketch these obsequies for another
small, quenched, unrepeatable spark.

4 February 1992

Eirlys

Running down to winter the vines
put on a last spurt
tendril towards the sun
light harvesting, scrape October's
thin sky soup onto their green plates
and gorge before the first chill breath
fills their veins with dried blood.
Up with the larky radiocaster
I drive through morning twilight
past women statuesque at bus-stops
knowing I can't give a lift to them all.

Up betimes our foremothers, cycladic
thighs thickened by child bearing
and buttocky suet pudding
or spry draggletails, gran's army
of widows and those whose old men
weren't up to much, waited for trams
dreading winter's onset, out in the early dark
with stockings over their boots
to swab and flick a duster
before the office boys blew in
shooting their paper cuffs.

All over the world they are still rising
to slice snow from pavements
under my hotel window on a Moscow morning
clean carriages, polish boards for money
to walk over, wipe the seats
for other bums and flush, polish
the city's sole with elbow grease
and beeswax, holding back
disorder, the silting down of dust
time's and weather's fingerprint on sill.

Salvage

My mother's cutting-out shears were sacred.
I wasn't allowed to blunt their edge even
on pattern paper so flimsy it might
have been stuck on the sweet bottoms of macaroons
and be swallowed like secret messages.
I can see them now laid against the pattern edge
or the line from the grey coin of chalk that darkened
where I put my tongue tip, and the wooden
table top that had to be recovered with its
newspaper cloth for tea, and hear them carving
upper to lower with that unmistakable
grind against the wood, decisive, no going back,
the full length of the blades, those jaws

too heavy in her bony fingers that held them
steady as a gun to the shoulder. They trimmed me
to my shape, snipped off my dry selvedges,
though others later pinned and tacked, eased a seam or two.
It was her wielding of the shears, not those
she sometimes used that let fall triangular
soft confetti, small silk sails, tweed spores, black
beauty spots in serge, pinked out, but the fatal
severers that ground away what I must work with.
And I've been gathering ever since, shortening
or lengthening hems and cuffs to get
a proper fit, something I can walk out in
not off the peg, ready made, but tailored
as she called herself, her trade, closing the metal
jaws resonant across the table top.

Ogres and Augurs

Now when I really need her the tooth fairy
doesn't come any more to leave a thruppenny joey
or bright tanner under my pillow
augur of a sharp ivory wedge chiselling its way
up from the bone. Instead those childhood ogres
Snaggletooth and Gummy Adams beckon from the shadows.
My sibilants shush like dragged feet through leaf mast
or the tide going out over shingle.
By the time I'm one with Yorick there'll be
hardly a peg for the archaeologists
to hang a date on. My imagination cries 'Pah!'
Yet I've done half as well again as my mother
whose new National Health dentures I gummed
to her forty-year-old jaw with a well-meant
toffee. Yesterday in the news I saw
a mugged man my age dubbed elderly.
But how can that be when I'm reading Goethe
for the first time and this morning, leaving you
I drove between hills sugared with rime
and hollows brimming with mist white as milk teeth?

A Sunday Outing

'I knew if anyone could find me out you would.'
Your cracked lips force the words through, bloody drop by drop.
I say 'I'm sorry. Hope you don't mind.' I know you're proud:
a private person who never quite came out, always on top

except with one or two, including me. It takes
one to know one. Today I've driven through weeping rain
and howling wind to find you here; past infernal lakes
the season fills from every open city vein.

The gaunt old hospital's about to close; the new postmodernist
gleams in brick and tile but no one sleeps there yet.
Instead it's still this seamy block, the scabrous lift
that hauls me up alone to an unmarked floor where I'm met

a little curiously, I think. The nurses' eyes
outshine in semi-precious jet or opal; tongues soothe
with creole and blarney. Yet their smiles can't disguise
the bagged bones the masseur comes with gentle touch to
    smooth.

I turn the corner and see you lying so flat it's as if
they've let out all your air. Or like the pictures in the Tate
they were queuing for as I drove past: no third dimension, no
    relief
plain pain, sans serif. Mortality's at best a dodgy state.

But here there's love enough to break your heart.
I take your hand. This thin the wrist bends back on a bone
Hansel might have thrust through the caging bars. We don't
    know how to part.
Instead I ask and hear how long you've known.

Legend II

They aren't at all as we've imagined them
these events at the top of the tall house
whose lower rooms dealt in import and export
invoice and ledger and bill of sale
between the duck dipped canals.
It's the father who comes back
Ulysses to us, wagging an old dog's tail
thump, thump of recognition and hope
not knowing his wife, children, friends
have all charred in Moloch's gullet.
We watch with him while hope gutters out.

History is at best fiction, what we choose
to pluck and preserve. There were eight people
up there, terrified or resigned
the ugly, the undesired, the peevish
the Lazarus who returned
to a life still sepultured.

'Of the girls who died, most of them Trojan
from rape and the sword, we remember
Iphigenia who greased the slipway
with wine-dark bubbles dashed from her maid's veins.'
Myth cleanses history of slime and terror and ash.

And those who stripped to their blond skins
to bathe in Phlegeton, trusting
Persephone would bring them
pomegranates to suck to the domed husk
(with thin red juice running down their chins
as they licked their fingers of immortality)
time's flushed them away too, leaving
this icon of a schoolgirl bent
over her diary, and each of us
murderer and preserver running up the stairs
while we beg the huntsman not to cut out
Snow White's heart as the pencil whispers
an older story: 'Once upon a time
there was a princess. The wolf ate her.'

STEPHEN ROMER

Stephen Romer was born in Hertfordshire in 1957 and educated at Cambridge and Harvard. He has lived much of his adult life in France, first in Paris and now in Tours, where he is Maître de Conférences at the University. He published three collections of poetry with OUP: *Idols* (1986), *Plato's Ladder* (1992) and *Tribute* (1998). He has translated widely from modern French poetry, notably Yves Bonnefoy and Jacques Dupin. He contributed to the English translation of Paul Valéry's *Cahiers* (Peter Lang, 2001), and his *Choice of Twentieth-century French verse* is due from Faber in Spring 2002.

A Refuge in Benares

You again in dreams on waking
you at sunrise and at sundown
over the flat grey Ganges

I sat among the mutton bones
under the bougainvillea, in the grove
where Krishnaji would come
and preach the perfect mental freedom
of *now* of *now* of *now*

Your body gleamed,
a perpetual burning in the mind's eye

There was a dog's carcass
jammed in a cleft
its head hanging down in the water
its rump upended
swaying obscenely in the current

It met me on my daily walk,
at my going out and my coming in.
No one ever touched it:
my eyes were fixed upon my feet

And to test him the Lord Maitreya
Became a gangrenous mongrel
And the Bhiku knelt
To lick the maggots off it with his tongue.
And the mongrel became the Lord Maitreya,
He raised his hand in blessing . . .

On the Buddha's path, the melancholy path
to Sarnath, I sickened and turned back

Downriver from the bodyburning
I filled a little phial
with saffron flower and cholera
to print on your forehead:
my token of farewell

The journey back
was a particled blackness
inlaid with eyes and embers.
A stick of charcoal
broken in the nose and throat

I grew to dread
the road-rail bridge,
Iron Malaviya, Malaviya Jagganath,
clamouring to the East
with the permanence of Hell,
a devourer of souls
a spreader of contagion

In dreams on waking
at sunrise and at sundown
I heard the Malaviya
grinding men

And often in the shuttered bungalow
curled on my bed
I gave the whole thing up,
the shadowy Compassion.
Somewhere near delirium
I fell towards your body like a stone.

The Baker's Shop

The baker's shop is warm,
sweet-smelling,
a single room
of whitewashed stone,
clean swept
and quite bare.
Mid-afternoon,
the oven mouth is sealed.
A rough wood table
holds the floor

and a cabinet
with nothing in it
lounges one-leggedly
against a wall.
That wooden shovel
propped in a corner
is the oar of Odysseus:
the rascal
swagged the loaves
and scarpered,
not a minute since,
leaving by the window
that stands wide open
on a landfall
of lemon and rogue olive.

The Join

At the water's muddied edge
we halt and watch
the meeting of river and sky

marked by a rope of gulls
rising in a body
that scatters, widens, contracts,

the heart in the echograph
our vitals jumping into focus
like death on the screen

that fixture in the distance
on the hinge of forty,
the placid-implacable slide

to the join. This is the prospect,
the vertiginous horizontal.
Pink and pale-blue, with violet wavelets

further out, sister and brother
standing with absences beside us
unspoken but there,

mortal panic meeting head-on
with indestructible longing
and unkillable joy . . .

Loners
turning back to the car
the asphalt slick with ice

helpless to help
your advice to me:
Let the love flow outwards and away . . .

And mine to you:
May you not put yourself wholly
into unsafe hands!

Avenue Mozart

By now he's hurrying
as much towards his past
as into the future
though brought up short
by the lined and fretful face
in a shopfront (*he should
see himself!*) a bouquet

in his sweaty palm, head turning
like a marionette at every
down-&-shadow girl
who comes a-floating
intent on the carriage
of her impeccable breasts,
the staple idiom of France:

créer une zone de turbulence
that lingerie ad
of a cambered back and buttocks
still perks him up
after all these years
there's lime-fluff in the air
he's cock of the walk

among *tout ce petit monde*
of butchers and bakers
and small-time tobacconists
with stacks of fresh newsprint
the city new-minted
and furnished forth
all flowers and starch

a table laid
it seems for him
turning into a doorway
and up six aching floors
to a locked door
and a note.
(Does he read the word *pity*?)

With the petulant spasm
of tears and shame
comes recognition,
the roué collapsed
by the stinking fountain
in a rictus of derision
– *Beware! Beware!*

the powder, the rouge,
the painted hair!
They're not far off,
on the hinge of forty
they're right on cue
so be beginning
to despair!

It's all the same
but later –
and none of it
gets easier –
when the new start
is a déjà vu, and beauty,
beauty looks straight through you.

Re-reading: Under the Volcano
– 'the dark's spinets . . .'

I can't reach the end – but draw it out, put it off,
defer, postpone, delay the last mescal, and reflect:
the drink situation was now this, was this . . .

Turn back! I can't kill him off quite yet –
momentito – what had he been saying?
Just more of his erudite gorgeous talk

to get drunk on, in a narrow bed,
in a shipwrecked crow's-nest nice and snug,
high above the city, some Indian flophouse

where the rats scurry, and persistent
phlegmy coughing and a slamming toilet door
is all there is of sleep; then the dawning fear

of being, this time, truly out of reach,
– *You've really done it now,* go the voices,
there's nothing on earth we can do for you!

– but not having to face it yet, not having
to face anything, for as long as the Consul hangs
upside down, oddly, in the turning wheel . . .

N.S. THOMPSON

N.S. Thompson was born in Manchester in 1950 and educated at Oxford, where he now teaches. His publications include the comparative study *Chaucer, Boccaccio and the Debate of Love* (1996) and a volume of poems *The Home Front* (1997). He is also active as a critic and translator.

Some of the poems in this anthology, or earlier versions of them, first appeared in *Oxford Magazine, New Orleans Review* (USA), *PN Review, Sewanee Theological Review* (USA) and *The Home Front*.

The Questions of Boeotia

How can we best use wintertime and spring
So as to earn our rest in summer, when
Artichokes ripen and the cicala sings?
When fat kids and our temperate cups refresh
Us – sunscorched workers in the dusty fields?
When should we start to reap the corn, pick beans?
When should the wagon's axle-tree be made?
Which is the best wood for plough-tail or pole?
How are the cattle best kept fit for work?
What method should we use for drying grapes?
But most of all, which are the lucky days,
The days when all our country work is blessed?
And which unlucky, when we should refrain?

These are the questions in Boeotia.

A Scent of Pines

I
      Circling round the Circus Maximus,
Alfas cruise for sex-slaves; evening pines
      Parasol Imperial Palatine,
  Shades cast on one last tourist bus.

II
      Girls in strip invade the pitch in teams,
Taking corners, tattooed ankles bare,
      Promising the grinding round of cars
  A wealth of personal regimes.

III
      Ghosts of track days over, now the whips
Springing his way from Rome's satirists,
      Caius feels round archways for a wrist
  To work those monumental hips.

The Girls

Le Cascine, Florence

I

All thigh boots, wigs and fluttered lashes, time
On hand, they wait there for the pantomime,
A ragged chorus hindlegged in the parks,
Oblivious to traffic or remarks,
Tossed out of windows; looking quite perverse,
They perch on top of bonnets to rehearse
For roles they ultimately must provide
By leisurely taking no one for a ride,
But sit and smoke and banter, more to please
Themselves than any tart desire to tease.

A Fiat Uno in the sunset skates
From outstretched leg to leg and contemplates
Them coolly, but receives a hard return
Of stares and trailing wisps of smoke that spurn
The early worm. Reluctant to procure,
It seems, these mime-artistes of pleasure lure
Clients only when they have them at their beck
And call, when cruising bodies battle neck
And neck, horns blaring in the sticky heat,
Night's show made satisfyingly complete.

II

Plane trees stage scant support, the masque-like scene
Develops: painted figures flaunt, obscene,
Unblinking as, from neon watchtowers, lamps
Cast shafts on concentrated labour camps,
The women pinned inside a golden cage
With timeless youth trapped next to timeless age;
And stuck there till the small hours, cigarettes
Alight, first one girl, then another, lets
Her body slide towards its destined end;
Through broken bars of light the rest descend.

When locking horns and squealing tyres attract
Attention of a sort, the final act
Comes with a litany but little grace;
Girls haggling time, protection or whose place
Are drawn towards the steady headlight beams
Like moths and flutter stupidly. What seems
To be on offer? Flesh that will entice
For anyone prepared to pay the price.
Cars lift them from the heartless orbs in swarms,
All night without applause each girl performs.

Anecdote of an Opus

When asked about his fine relief, Perseverus
Would dumbly scratch his palms and mutter 'Twenty years . . .'
                                                        to us,
His mind still bent by cornice, frieze or tympanum,
The last poised slabs of fine provincial *omnium gatherum*
Winched ready into place before they hit the street
With heads hacked off, the fresh wet dead that made the sack
                                                    complete.
Half-blind, he gratefully stumps where Rhea's arm supports
A roof-beam for the hovel Severinus' widow sports,
His Jove now hers, face one-eyed in a gaping wall,
The flat trunk buttressing. He knows all art is functional
And feels his way along. One day the Goths would come,
He knew, but itched to bring them down from pedestals in Rome.

Aqua Mirabilis

That term, school let us slip out to the deep
End, only ones to swing the baths for games,
And, well advised, we took off casually,
The sixth form thinking we were only friends.

Aqua mirabilis, aquamarine
Aquarium. We swam like two bright fish
Through opalescent waters patched with light,
Amphibian legs sleek in their element

And made waves, innocently, bobbing up
And down, cold noses nearly touching. Coup
Against school's flat iron fields, we could fish
Love's gleaming scale, bodies aquamarine,

Our touching feet twined as an element
Until we flopped, exhausted, dripping light
Diminished in dark cubicles. As friends
Again we took the turnstile casually,

An ache so different from those left by games
Now ending, as we bobbed along the deep
Streets, heads lit up still swimming from the coup,
And wondered would friends ever catch us up.

The Remedy

Feeling the pinch as she did must have hurt
    Her quiet perfection; skin and bone
Her line of study; body honed she drew
    The line at mixing, dined alone

And brought an air of mystery with her. Pots
    Of yoghurt missing, then a spoon
Of honey or some healthfood cereal gone . . .
    Nothing to lose sleep over. Soon

As down, she brought the lot up in remorse
      Then rinsed out guilt with whisky neat.
But as she never bothered much with food
      No one suspected her starved feet

Which wandered each night down to neighbours' shelves,
      While in the rooms her garments' arms
Stretched urgent gestures beyond help or love.
      The annexe slept, ignored alarms.

Till one night, medicated suds run for
      Her clean up, wrists blue with the cold,
She opened them to water's hug and left
      A body, fed up with its hold.

PETER HOWARD

Peter Howard was born in Nottingham in 1957, and educated at the Royal Grammar School, Worcester, and Hertford College, Oxford. His poems have appeared in various publications, including *Poetry Review, The Rialto, The Independent,* and *The Faber Book of Christmas*, and have been broadcast on Channel 4 Television. His short collection *Low Probability of Racoons* was published by Envoi Poets Publications in 1994. He won second prize in the 2000 *Daily Telegraph* / Arvon competition.

Of the poems in this anthology, π was first published in the *Snakeskin* webzine; *This is a No Smoking Zone* was first published in *The Cambridge Insider*; *Rubric* was first published in the 1996 *Bluenose Poets Anthology*; *The Yromem* and *Strangers* were first published in *Oxford Magazine* and *Word of Honour* was first published in *Orbis*.

Reticulating Splines

The scenery is screen, keyboard,
mug of neglected coffee,
fug and frustration.

The program explains
it's busy reticulating splines.
(Sub-text: this is complex, high-tech stuff.)

But *reticulating*
means making nets. *Spline* is an
East Anglian word

for a lath, or thin strip of wood.
Dour, bearded fen tigers pose
for an early photograph before

turning back to wrest
sparse livelihoods from a bleak land
under a wide sky.

π

I used to twist men round my little finger.
They wanted me to be simple
to fit their idea of aesthetics
but I was a coquette. I trailed
an infinite series of decimal places
behind me like a wedding dress
and wouldn't lie down and be a proper fraction:
no square pegs for me. I got around:
diversified into magnetism, flirted with statistics,
insinuated myself everywhere.
I'm embarrassed to let you see me come to this:
raised to that upstart's power, multiplied
by a clown I seriously doubt the existence of,
the result a cheap trick, worth less than nothing.

The Distillation of Ink

This is the Bunsen burner. By twisting
the collar we control how much air
is introduced to the stream

of unburned gas. Note
the cone of light and the
roaring sound when the hole

is fully opened. We do not need
such a fierce flame for this experiment.
You have already clamped

the flask of ink in place, connected
the Liebig's condenser with its sheath
of water to cool the condensate.

You have carefully positioned the beaker
at the lip of the delivery tube.
Now, gently heat the ink

until it begins to boil.
You would not have thought
it could be separated from

its seemingly innate blueness.
Yet here, slowly appear
drops that trickle

down: refugees from a war zone,
deracinated, shorn of possessions
and identity, absolutely clear.

This is a No Smoking Zone

Spontaneous combustion causes serious
disease, can lead to loss of life. Your own's
your business, but our rules are not 'imperious',
'intrusive', as you claim. We need these zones
because the secondary effects, disputed
though they may be, are still of great concern
to many. And it cannot be refuted:
this is a growing problem. You must learn
to burn in private, you who are less fortunate,
less (dare I say) enlightened. Keep your gods
away from thunderbolts. If we're importunate,
it's for the common good. Silk, amber rods,
and cats don't mix. Don't try it. Keep the hatches
shut fast when not in use. Don't play with matches.

Rubric

Do not take anything with you into the examination.
You have limited, but unspecified time to complete it.
The invigilator is not authorised to give any assistance.
Good answers to a few questions are no better
than a large number of fragmentary answers,
but do not be disheartened.
Do the best you can.
Show all steps in your reasoning.

Do not attempt to bribe the examiner.
However, gold and silver vessels,
black cockerels, virgins, palm leaves,
taxes on the just and unjust alike,
repressed sexuality, scourges, massacres of
innocents, burnt offerings (excepting humans,
which come under a different category),
ecstatic states, incense, prostration,

the shaving of hair or its remaining
unscissored, likewise fingernails and foreskins,
are subject to special consideration,
on their individual merits.

Continue until you are told to stop.
If you think you have finished before then,
you are mistaken.
Do not take anything out of the room when you leave.
You will not be permitted to re-enter once you have left.
The examination has already started.
May we take this opportunity of wishing you the best of luck.

You are going to need it.

The Yromem

We envy you, with your backwards
facing memories, the future always
a bright birthday surprise.

Ours work forwards, always will do
and presumably, always have.
The advantages are superficial:

no such thing as an unexpected guest,
no need to wonder if we'll run out of butter,
and although we rarely lose our way

(since we know the turning
as we approach each cross-roads)
we never know why we came or from where.

Insurance firms have an easy time,
but a whodunnit holds little fascination,
and the National Lottery was not a success.

There are professors of clairvoyance
at every university; historians
occupy tents at the fairgrounds

our children run to, bright
with the memory of the rides they'll take,
always returning downcast.

We mourn their birth, for then
their lives erode, as years slip
into the unknowable past.

We still fear death.

Strangers

Do they draw ritual symbols beneath the living room carpet,
have one pierced nipple, eat eggs raw
including the shells? Do they shop at four in the morning

for catfood and longlife batteries, but would never,
ever buy ricotta cheese or pastrami?
What about their holidays?

Perhaps they spend them, every one,
at the same B&B locked up in their rooms all day, while the sun
flays a beach you can't see from the window.

Are they scared of heights and horseshoes, but crunch spiders
when they can get them? Do they spend hours reading histories
of matchstick distribution, writing letters to the editor,

deciding whether to peel an orange? If a bus ran over them
what would they be wearing underneath? If you opened their
    cupboards
would you find pictures they'd painted thirty years ago, stolen
    locks of hair,

a dead wasp in a plastic box? Do they listen at night
for the small sounds that might contain an answer? When you see
    them
huddled around the table in the back room of the pub, are their
    voices

murmuring incantations, or coded messages concerning
secret missions, things you will never know of unless
they happen to involve you, and even then, only when it is too
    late?

Word of Honour

Nothing I say is true. Your eyes are not
Like mist upon the moor. You're never late.
Your mind is not a box of jewels. The spate
Of rivers has no bearing. You aren't hot
As coins in a child's hand, a shot
Of something strong, the ribbons at a fête.
There are no fireworks. Things aren't so great.
Our fragile love is shrinking to the dot
On old-time turned-off TV sets. I wish
You'd change, be worthy of me. I regret
That you can't dance or sing. It's all untrue:
One in a million, tiny silver fish,
Caged bird, my secret forest. You don't set
Me skywards on champagne. I don't love you.

PETER SCUPHAM

Peter Scupham was born in Liverpool in 1933 and educated at The Perse, Cambridge and St George's, Harpenden. After National Service he went to Emmanuel College, Cambridge, where he read English. He has taught, lectured, run a private press with John Mole, and now sells second-hand books, writes, and, with Margaret Steward, produces Shakespeare in their Norfolk garden. Recent books of poetry from Oxford University Press include *The Air Show* (1988), *Watching the Perseids* (1990) and *Selected Poems* (1990). His latest collection, *Night Watch* (1999) was published by Anvil Press and his *Collected Poems* is due out in 2003. He is a Fellow of the Royal Society of Literature.

Look up the Chimney

The master sweep and his ginger boy
go into their double-act: chaff, grins
and a pother of indoor fireworks
conjure us to pry beyond ourselves
into a dry womb, a dark lantern.
Huge, soft webs of best-forgotten
spread and sigh behind the painted wall

and families become familiars gather,
fleshed out in stuff we try to think for them:
cooked smells heavy as old money,
hours of dimmish talk, heat
which seeps a little into worsted flesh.
Night, pushed some inches further back,
shawls about to force an entrance

against the updraught of our voices
as they climb a stairway to the stars,
scour that blackened lung which draws breath
in and ever in, coughing, spluttering
over the childish wishes that we posted
and watched reduced to negatives
or floated on to God and Father Christmas

confabulating in their empty nests,
each smoky head crowned with coals of fire.
The sweep's brush is at its rat-scratch;
shock-headed Peter breaks his finger-nails,
chokes above a flaring sheaf of straw,
gnawed to a cancer in slypes and wynds
where time ciphers its ash messages.

The Map Maker

The sound of paper – surely that's the same?
Open it out. Sprung on my finger-ends
the resistance is purposive, a clean flip.
On the obverse, four spots of glue hold nothing, tightly,
their ochres caked and crystalline. He spreads it out
as I spread it now, smoothing its awkward lie.
Folds guide small rivulets of shade, flats cream
under gaslight or whiten in the profligate sun.

This is how he sees it. Rather, how what he sees
in the beck, the lane, the heat-haze over the wolds
can be dried and certified, held like moths
in his killing-bottle. Catlike, he marks his journey.
Ink runs thinly, darkens. He sows words broadcast,
dips, the scratch-pen, straight-edges the railway
as, outside, hot verges coarsen with umbellifers.
Lineside. Tiger beetles, flowers. Lepidoptera in general.

His head adrift with flutterings, sheen and texture,
he pushes his way through millions of green and brown,
holding tight to a spinning signpost of names.
His tracks race off the paper through *Nova Scotia*.
J. Scupham July 9, 1916. In brightest Lincolnshire
my twelve-year-old father carefully encodes
Hill, Clearing, Viper's Bugloss, Yellow Underwings,
ransacks *America* for its *Heaths* and *Tigers* –

the Large Heath, (*Epinephele Tithonus*),
the Scarlet Tiger, (*Callimorpha Dominula*) –
This Midsummer, his 'Prize for Nature Study'
is Furneaux' *British Butterflies and Moths.*
With bruised laurel, cyanide of potassium,
the countryside may be coaxed into your trap
and, later, secured by silver, black or gilded pins.
Be sure the poison does not merely stupefy,

leaving you horrified, when your box is opened,
'by the sight of the poor victim struggling to free itself',
a teeming landscape unwilling to lie down.
I refold his paper, packed with nests and burrows,

thickets of skin and fur. Ink and copy-pencil
shine briefly against my lamp, keep the dry glaze
lost by close on a hundred years of eyes.
The dead rustle back to nest with a stir of wings;

the annular rings thicken and simplify.
I could stand there still, lost in a no-man's-land,
holding his childhood's trench-map, think of his brother
laying his gun-sights somewhere on the Somme,
consider how folds of dead ground foster rivulets,
hedges whiten to blackthorn, cream to hawthorn.
As he dies, I ask how he spends his time,
bedbound. 'Oh, just go for walks,' he answers.

Flight into Egypt

Some who were warned in dreams to pack and go
across a hasty line ruled in the sand,
found scrub and mirage at the rainbow's end,
the tombs of strangers in occluding snow
and unmade promises in promised land.

Trapped in the cruel nonsenses of things,
they learned their guiding star a marker flare
which drew more darkness down upon their fear;
died by their neighbours' knives, or under blades
whirled into plague about the ice-bound air.

And innocence, which lived a day, then died,
sighs in the ebb-voice of a broken wave
how this one child was cupboarded by love
until his flesh grew ripe, then crucified
by those whose childhood was an open grave.

Estuary

Myriads of stones knock their heads together,
chatterboxing under that mew, mew, mew.
Come clean to this confluence of waters;
turn your back on the loneliness of windows
and, sick as Lazarus with his single death,
feel for life, the hauling in, the ebb of it

where slips of tide follow their own creases
this way, that way, by a crooked gantry
signifying loss, which has its own nine bouges,
its own bedevillings. These wraiths of sea-mist
nibble the heart out, have a cunning
to sting your fingers to crossed purposes,

reveal no more than shallow stains of lichen
hooped by rust, your softened footprints.
As marram grass keens about this Golgotha,
let the spilt brains of weed and bladderwrack
show you the separations of the self
and the frost wind take your bearings

off out to sea, beating an iron drum
of half-sunk cogs which snap at nothing.
Pay out and further out your lines of thought,
hear wind and water sing – if you can bear the burden
which thrills through blocks, and baulks and wires
littered on the shifting, shiftless sand –

of how the sea bobs with familiar faces:
the dead you rescued and the dead you drowned,
how, to the landward of your field of vision,
breed further fluctuations of the hour:
the outstretched hands you long ago let slip,
the loving voices which would call you home.

The Old Type Tray
for Roger Burford Mason, 1943–1998

Here triune orchid, Caesar, swan,
find Auden's common box, lie down
in beds of loose and lettered gravel;
Patience now must undishevel
  feathers, tongues and petals long dispelled –
  the case is everything which is the world.

Collected Works, Principia,
primal scream and earliest ur,
tall talk, the latest from the street
where Caliban, Miranda meet
  spill from his crazy leaden casket, still
  packed to the brim with hope and syllable.

For words – which grew from thinginess –
have cast their spells in metal dress,
each petalled, feather-light impression
a stay against their distribution:
  typographer and text, the clock defied,
  put to their final proof, and justified.

ANTHONY HECHT

Anthony Hecht was born in New York City in 1923. He was educated at Columbia University and is married with three children. He has published eight volumes of poetry, of which the latest is *The Darkness and the Light*. He is also the author of three volumes of essays and criticism; a fourth, to be called *Melodies Unheard*, is forthcoming.

Of the poems in this anthology, 'Despair' first appeared in *Pivot*; 'Illumination' appeared in *The New Yorker* and 'Long-Distance Vision' was first published in the *Hudson Review*.

Despair

Sadness. The moist grey shawls of drifting sea-fog,
Salting scrub-pine, drenching the cranberry bogs,
Erasing all but foreground, making a ghost
Of anyone who walks softly away;
And the faint, penitent psalmody of the ocean.

Gloom. It appears among the winter mountains
On rainy days. Or the tiled walls of the subway
In caged and ageing light, in the steel scream
And echoing vault of the departing train,
The vacant platform, the yellow destitute silence.

But despair is another matter. Mid-afternoon
Washes the worn bank of a dry arroyo,
Its ochre crevices, unrelieved rusts,
Where a startled lizard pauses, nervous, exposed
To the full glare of relentless, marigold sunshine.

The Hanging Gardens of Tyburn

Mysteriously fed by the dying breath
Of felons, by the foul odour that melts
Down from their bodies hanging on the gallows,
The rank, limp flesh, the soft pendulous guilts,

This solitary plant takes root at night,
Its tiny charnel blossoms the pale blue
Of Pluto's ice pavilions; being dried,
Powdered and mixed with the cold morning dew

From the left hand of an executed man,
It confers untroubled sleep, and can prevent
Prenatal malformations if applied
To a woman's swelling body, except in Lent.

67

Take care to clip only the little blossoms,
For the plant, uprooted, utters a cry of pain
So highly pitched as both to break the eardrum
And render the would-be harvester insane.

Illumination

Ground lapis for the sky, and scrolls of gold,
Before which shepherds kneel, gazing aloft
At visiting angels clothed in egg-yolk gowns,
Celestial tinctures smuggled from the East,
From sunlit Eden, the palmed and plotted banks
Of sun-tanned Aden. Brought home in fragile grails,
Planted in England, rising at Eastertide,
Their petals cup stamens of topaz dust,
The powdery stuff of cooks and cosmeticians.
But to the camels-hair tip of the finest brush
Of Brother Anselm, it is the light of dawn,
Gilding the hems, the sleeves, the fluted pleats
Of the antiphonal archangelic choirs
Singing their melismatic *pax in terram*.
The child lies cribbed below, in bestial dark,
Pale as the tiny tips of crocuses
That will find their way to the light through drifts of snow.

Long-Distance Vision

How small they seem, those men way in the distance.
Somehow they seem scarcely to move at all,
    And when they do it is slowly,
Almost unwillingly. I bend my head
To my writing, look up half an hour later,
    And there they are, as if

Engaged in boring discussion, fixed in a world
Almost eventless, where it is somehow always
    Three in the afternoon,
The best part of the day already wasted,
And nothing to do till it's time for the first drink
    Of the uneventful evening.

I know, of course, binoculars would reveal
They are actually doing something – one doubles over,
    (Is it with pain or laughter?)
Another hangs his jacket on the handle
Of his bicycle, tucks in his Versace sportshirt
    And furtively checks his fly.

But the naked eyesight smooths and simplifies,
And they stand as if awaiting the command
    Of a photographer
Who, having lined them up in a formal group,
Will tell them to hold even stiller than they seem
    Till he's ready to dismiss them.

In much the same way, from a palace window,
The king might have viewed a tiny, soundless crowd
    On a far hill assembled,
Failing to see what a painter would have recorded:
The little domes, immaculate in their whiteness,
    At the foot of the cross.

The Ceremony of Innocence

He was taken from his cell, stripped, blindfolded,
And marched to a noisy room that smelled of sweat.
Someone stamped on his toes; his scream was stopped
By a lemon violently pushed between his teeth
And sealed with friction tape behind his head.
His arms were tied, the blindfold was removed
So he could see his tormentors, and they could see
The so much longed for terror in his eyes.
And one of them said, 'The best part of it all
Is that you won't even be able to pray.'
When they were done with him, two hours later,
They learned that they had murdered the wrong man.
And this made one of them thoughtful. Some years after,
He quietly severed connections with the others,
Moved to a different city, took holy orders,
And devoted himself to serving God and the poor.
But the intended victim continued to live
On a walled estate, sentried around the clock
By a youthful, cellphone-linked Praetorian Guard.

I.M.E.M.

To spare his brother from having to endure
Another agonising bedside vigil
With sterile pads, syringes but no hope,
He settled all his accounts, distributed
Among a few friends his most valued books,
Weighed all in mind and heart and then performed
The final, generous, extraordinary act
Available to a solitary man,
Abandoning his translation of Boileau,
Dressing himself in a dark well-pressed suit,
Turning the lights out, lying on his bed,
Having requested neighbours to wake him early
When, as intended, they would find him dead.

70

LUCY NEWLYN

Lucy Newlyn was born in Uganda in 1956. She grew up in Leeds, and took her first and second degrees in English at Lady Margaret Hall, Oxford. She became a Fellow of St Edmund Hall in 1986, where she teaches English Literature. Her publications include *Coleridge, Wordsworth and the Language of Allusion* (OUP, 1986), *Paradise Lost and the Romantic Reader* (OUP, 1993) and *Reading Writing and Romanticism: The Anxiety of Reception* (OUP, 2000). Her most recent book has been awarded a Rose Mary Crawshay prize by the British Academy. Having spent her entire career teaching and writing about poetry, she started writing it herself only a year ago. Some of her poems have been published in the *Oxford Magazine*, including 'Your Lost Poem', which is reprinted here. She is married, with a daughter and two step-children.

Anniversary
14 December 2000

No snow came soundlessly
on this non-day
from nowhere strangely

bringing muffled voices
and treacherous bouquets
draped in cellophane.

How you hated
(freesias the one exception)
these corpses fed on water and aspirin,

roses for visiting
lilies for burying
tulips for remembering:

a good show,
like the see-through coffin
you wore your best velvet in.

All the long morning
was your winding-sheet unwinding
your body lifted from linen.

All afternoon
an immense bowl
of empty floodlit now

filling steadily with then
in slow motion
and then again.

Your Lost Poem

No comparison
but I'm drawn to making one
with the black sack

I witnessed on a screen:
nothing inside it, not a single track
or trace to say the life had ever been.

Nothing can stop you knowing
and of course you know
it must have come adrift by now

scattered abroad
to the four winds and blown
about like thistledown.

Watch closely though
in a cleft between two rocks, a hollow,
your new poem in embryo.

Beads

Imagine a necklace
with no two beads alike,
and threaded by a child.

It's not spaced evenly,
light-dark, light-dark,
in a predictable pattern.

It doesn't move smoothly
in a perfect circle –
small to big and back again.

It has a golden clasp,
but the thread is elastic,
and the first beads are tacky.

They give way to a chunkier style:
weathered conkers and oak-apples,
East African wood and ivory,

then a stretch of glass baubles,
some smooth and round like marbles
some multifaceted, like precious jewels.

Next there's a sudden bright flash
of pink and magenta and terra-cotta –
hand painted clay, Malaysian,

followed by a loop of lapis
alongside warm amber, then sombre
jet, and pearls like tears.

No two beads alike,
each one telling a story.
Another's added today.

Wear this necklace for each other
on your anniversary:
forty-eight beads long,

forty-eight beads strong,
and getting longer, stronger.
A half-century is only two beads away.

Nearly a Sonnet:
for Suzy, after a reunion and shopping

You keep appearing and reappearing
In greys and browns and blues –
Each time more elegant, more sophisticated,
More filmy and flowing than the last,
And reflected from three different angles:
Once in the mirror alongside you, once
In the mirror in front of you, and once again
In a mirror down the hallway to our past.

From the outside looking in,
It was the designer-silks we saw.
But now we're here, inside this metaphor,
It's clear that you are what we came in
Looking for. Every time your image
Disappears, I catch you reappearing,
Just as you always were: the same slight form,
The same muddle of curls, as irrepressible
As your bubbling, high-pitched laughter.
Let it be always so: you are changeless amid all
The changing, with no before and after.

CHARLES TOMLINSON

Charles Tomlinson was born in Stoke-on-Trent in 1927 and was educated at Queens' College, Cambridge, where he is now an Honorary Fellow. He began teaching at Bristol University in 1956 and is now Emeritus Professor and a Senior Research Fellow there. He has published more than twenty volumes of poetry, including a *Selected Poems, 1955–1997* (OUP) and his most recent volume, *Vineyard Above the Sea* (Carcanet, 1999). In addition, he has written, with Octavio Paz, two books of collaborative poems, *Renga* and *Airborn*, and was recently invited to Japan to participate in the first nationally sponsored collaborative *Renshi* with leading Japanese poets.

He has translated widely from the Spanish poetry of Antonio Machado, Cesar Vallejo and Octavio Paz, from the Russian of Pushkin and Tyutchev and from the Italian, including most recently, a *Selected Poems of Attilio Bertolucci*. He edited *The Oxford Book of Verse in English Translation* and *Eros English'd: Classical Erotic Poetry in Translation*. His Clark Lectures were published as *Poetry and Metamorphosis* (CUP).

He has edited the selected poems of William Carlos Williams, George Oppen and Octavio Paz as well as critical essays on Williams and Marianne Moore. A collection of his *American Essays* includes the re-issue of *Some Americans: a Personal Memoir* (Carcanet).

He has received the Cittadella Premio Europeo and a number of American poetry prizes, including the Joseph Bennett award in New York and was recently made an Honorary Foreign Fellow of the American Academy of Arts and Sciences and appointed a CBE. His work has been widely translated and several volumes of his poetry have appeared in Italy, Portugal, Mexico and Spain.

Keele University is recording a unique archive of all the poems of Tomlinson, read by himself.

In Ferrara

Carp the size of sheep
muscle their course to the surface
as they leap at the scraps of bread
flung their way. The concerted rush
raises a ripple, pushes back
the floating sediment
on this moat of the Estensi
and leaves a clear, clean space for play
over the beer-brown depths,
bellies glittering, disappearing.
It was energy like this
raised those walls, their height
filled with unfurnished emptiness now.
It is night. The street lamps
punctuate the alternation
of a depth-charge force and a dead calm
under this lavish scattering of bread.

Waiting for the Bus
at Tlacochahuaya

Goats
gnawing the prickly pears
with rock-hard jaws
lean between sand and spines
up into the bush. The crossroads
grow festive as we wait:
it is a subdued festivity
when the people of two villages
meet at a crossroads and kiss hands,
gathering into both their own
the hand to be kissed and with warmth
kiss it, saying softly
Qué tal? qué tal? The surprise
is a ritual surprise –
not so that of the two young men

79

who know each other yet did not know
both were travelling today
and to the same place – *Aah!* –
and having patted each other
they embrace, wandering side by side
absorbed in the fact of friendship.
A man leads three bulls
across the road, but no one
takes this in: they have eyes
only for humanity – the goats
are also invisible to them.
When we entered the village
a man on a burro had saluted us:
You are going to Tlacochahuaya?
We moved on through the *Buenos días*
of others and to the church
where a one-armed Indian
stood at the door and silent
gestured us inside, but this one-armed guide
neither guided nor begged.
Darkness, then the painted walls
covered with an angel army
– more cupids than angels:
the Dominicans had taught their flock
to paint them here
and unthrone Tlaloc (still tongued
in the village name)
and to convert the pagan gods
into saints and demons.
Two small girls followed us
as we left, asking
for *moni, moni, moni,*
merely murmuring the word.
We regained the crossroads
and the man on the burro, returning,
was it stated or enquired
You have been to Tlacochahuaya?
And now out of the dust
a bus that will carry us back
suddenly arrives and the conductor
reciting *Oaxaca, Oaxaca,*
begins to stow aboard

his restive customers until
they fill the interior
and, giving blow on blow
to the resonant metal of the vehicle,
conveys to the waiting *operador*
it is time to go.

from Lessons

1. *On a Picture of Burslem by Leonard Brammer*

He was that quiet man who taught us art –
Or rather left us to ourselves to learn.
I copied mannequins from Chirico
Hoping for recognition. Was it despair
Drove him to ignore his herd of boys?
'The self-taught man' – and that was us –
'Is taught by a very ignorant person.'
Constable said that. I saw it then,
As he issued sheets of paper, kept his peace.
There was no secret he would teach me
Although he knew them. Look at this thirties view.
It took me years to see that Stoke-on-Trent
Offered a theme for words. The waste, flat ground
Stretches behind roofs and bottle ovens,
And seems a lake beneath such pallid light,
All are on foot, the car not yet arrived.
He was a Lowry, not a Chirico man.
I'd traced the outlines and that didn't please him –
If only he had shown me how to draw.
This forgery of silhouettes was all he saw
And warned the class against, much to my shame,
Though being a decent, gentle sort of man
Blamed only 'someone', never spoke my name.

4. *In Memory of Agnes Beverley-Burton*

I did not learn to draw until that lady
(Not easy to please) saw my incompetence
At sketching trees and, Simplify, she said,
Follow only the leading lines of things,
And commandeered my hand to imitate
A cluster of boughs, then sped it on
To face another jutting ganglion
Where both eye and trunk were made to feel
The presence of a directed force, taught me to see
The heaves of structure up the entire tree
And plot its course from roots to summit
In whatever season, where the branches
Hung simplified by winter, simplified by leaves.

CARMEN BUGAN

Carmen Bugan was born in Romania in 1970 and emigrated to the United States with her family as political dissidents, after her father was released from prison. She studied literature and psychology at the University of Michigan – Ann Arbor. There she won a Hopwood Award and a Cowden Memorial Fellowship for her poetry. She later obtained an MA in poetry from Lancaster University and The Poets' House (Ireland). She is now working on a DPhil on the poetry of Seamus Heaney at Balliol College, Oxford. Her poems appeared in small newspapers and magazines in the United States, Ireland and Romania and she has read her work on Michigan Public Radio and other radio stations around Michigan.

Of the poems in this anthology, 'Fertile Ground' and 'The First Visit' were published in *The HazMat Review* Vol. 4; 'By the Lamp, Burning' was published in *Napalm Health Spa Report 2000* and 'Emilia' was published in *Cyphers #45*, Spring/Summer 1998.

Sleeping Apple

'I want to sleep the sleep of the apples'

Lorca

She dreams of how constellations
of apples turn in their sleep
towards stars in the silence
of the orchard.

I know she dreams:
she glows in the basket
nestled among blushing sisters.

Fertile Ground

I was pruning tomato plants when they came to search
for weapons in our garden;
they dug the earth under the chickens, bell peppers,
tiny melons, dill and horse-radishes.

I cried over sliced egg-plants
made one with the dirt,
over fresh-dug earth and morning glories.

Their shovels uncovered bottles
with rusted metal caps – sunflower cooking oil
my father kept for 'dark days', purchased in days equally dark.
Their eyes lit – everyone got a bottle or two –
a promise for their families' meals.

And when the oil spilled on the ground, shiny over crushed
     tomatoes
they asked me about weapons we might have kept.
'Oil,' I said: 'You eat and live.
This alone makes one dangerous.'

At her Funeral
for my grandmother

Villagers dressed in black lay bridges of cloth
from the living room to the carriage
and walk the coffin on their shoulders
over the threshold,
over the bed of chrysanthemums
she had looked at in the early mornings.

The mourners put their hands together
under the black ribbons above the doors,
and sing of her eyebrows turning into moss
her eyes turning into violets
her bones turning into flutes.

The Father leads the cortège to the church
with the book and three boys carrying flags.
They stop at every street corner
to make prayers of return into humid earth.

Here, in the horse-drawn carriage
she is a bride crossing the gate of the cemetery
behind a trail of incense and songs,
a wooden cross and a box filled with bread.
Hundreds of oak leaves whisper in the sun.
Her soul, like a vapour
joins the afternoon light
from mounds of flowers and lit candles.

The First Visit

The family went inside cement walls
in the centre of the town,
stood inside metal gates
in the centre of the prison,
and waited. Hours swelled
like the shadows of passing black trucks
loaded with *criminals*.

When they finished shaving him,
after they covered the wounds on his head with a cap,
there was a rumble of chains and keys.
His wife and children were taken to the visiting room;
'Twenty minutes,' the guard said.

Twenty minutes in August each year
twenty minutes –
a mouth full of suffering,
words swollen by microphones
sank into the thick wall of glass
between us.

Through two rooms, through two square holes in the walls
the little boy said: 'Daddy, I thought I'd bring you some apples.'

The Divorce

Before they brought him to the courtroom, they gave him three
    apples:
Your wife sent you these. He cradled each apple in the cup of his
    hands.
The smoothness of their skin became the cheeks of each child.

Inside the courthouse there was a quiet opening and closing of
    doors.
A crowd of people was chanting his name under the windows.
When the door of the divorce room opened, I saw his bare feet in
    brown shoes.

His children held each other tight against the wall.
Their breaths, white with cold, were rising towards the ceiling.
They listened for the voices of their parents.

When the divorce was over, he was allowed to see them:
they kissed his chained hands, promised to be good, let their tears
     fall
on his prison uniform with his own, all three of them burying him.

How I wished we could hide him with our bodies and take him
     home!
The Securitate peeled us off him. But we were the apple seeds left
     to grow
in the sound of his chains on the cement floor.

I Drink with You

When you knew that I was leaving
you bought me a pair of red shoes;
I left them in Florence with the memory of your hands.
You were unsure when you said: *so you'll dance and forget.*
October was pale in a bouquet of chrysanthemums.
For every year that I was gone you buried in the ground
one crimson bottle of wine. I never knew this –
how you felt when you gathered the sweetness of autumn
and hoped that its magic would call me back.
Now I touch the corners of your black scarf,
the white hair of your widow-braids. I kiss your hands
which rest on the wine stained tablecloth.

After Seven Years, for the Unearthing of your Body

Tomorrow they will open your grave:
your bones will sound against each other,

the voice of your hills lulls frozen grass
to rest, to rest, to rest in peace.

The Father will chant *Vesnica Pomenire*,
the family will feast on pilaf and grape leaves.

This Saturday your soul will take another journey;
I write to wish you light

from here, where the moon is stuck full to the window
white, unmerciful, sinking in curtains.

All night above the grave, everyone will sit with you
drinking the wine you pressed for this wake.

The church choir – all your friends – will sing,
and Grandmother will be there, in death as in life.

She waited for you nine years, dreaming in the ground
just as you waited, lighting incense at her head;

in spring, when you cleared the weeds from her grave
you thought of lying next to her, close to the train tracks.

'I like the train whistling' you said once
while we picked violets in the cemetery.

Since you died, you have returned to me three times:
once you were in my husband's dream,

once we sat on the balcony with the wind-lamp,
and last you held my hand in a poem.

Grandfather, I am in Ireland now, and tonight
they say the two worlds meet and speak to each other.

Arrive in a dream or a vision;
the fire is burning, I lit three candles

there are prayers turning in my sleep
and I listen to songs I learned away from home.

I don't know where home is
Grandfather.

By the Lamp, Burning

Today I untangled a butterfly from my hair –
by this light I imagine him again
yellow tangled in yellow –

For three days now I've spoken to no one.
Only fireflies light my way back to camp.

I have been aware of you:
the never touches beside the tent,
the torn off pages with the way
I did not take.

Emilia

When he corners Emilia in the kitchen
      and strikes her because the house is cold,
the thin white curtain in the small window
      breathes with the air of his arm, moving.
Next to the stove is a bundle of twigs
      she had stolen from the nearby woods.

He smells of coal and vodka,
      his face is the black which never washes off.
Today she slept with the baker for a loaf of bread
      she carried home under her armpit to keep warm;
she breaks it for her husband and her daughter
      and gathers the crumbs in a cloth napkin.

At night she bends over the family well
      to bring the stars closer.

At three in the morning
      she peels frost-bitten potatoes, opens a jar of eggplants,
makes linden tea to keep in the cupboard for medicine.
      When the breakfast is ready she hums to herself.

In the afternoon the alarm shrieks over the mountain,
      she takes her daughter to see who has died;
he is brought in a coal cart from the depths,
      head crushed, arms severed, both palms open.

The song of the dead grows on her cracked lips
      on the path to the garden, past the stork's nest,
just as she rehearsed it from the beginning
      of her life.